NATIONAL
GEOGRAPHIC

Return to
Titanic

PATHFINDER EDITION

By Susan E. Goodman

CONTENTS

Re

Pieces of the Past. *Rust clings to Titanic's bow, the pointed front of the ship.* OPPOSITE PAGE: *In 1912, this watch was found on the body of a passenger.*

rn to Titanic

Titanic was meant to be the biggest and best ship of her day. Then she sank in 1912. Yet she's still the most famous boat on Earth.

By
Susan E. Goodman

Sailing Into History.
Passengers stand along Titanic's stern, or back.

The Wonder Ship

On April 10, 1912, hundreds of people crowded onto a dock in England. They came to see the *Titanic* set off on her **maiden** voyage. What made the ship so special?

First of all, *Titanic* was the largest ship in the world. She was as long as four city blocks. Many people called her "the wonder ship." Others said *Titanic* was the best ship ever built. Some even believed she was too strong to sink!

That's not all. *Titanic* was also a floating palace. She was one of the first ships with a pool. She had fine wood and gold chandeliers.

As a result, some of the wealthiest people in the world were aboard the ship. They traveled on the upper **decks.** Poorer passengers and the crew lived on the decks below.

The first days of *Titanic*'s voyage toward New York were like a party. Passengers celebrated in grand fashion. They thought they were making history. They were right.

Danger Ahead!

Everything started out smoothly. By the 14th of April, *Titanic* was in the middle of the Atlantic Ocean. The weather was clear. That night, the stars glistened against the cold, dark sky.

Shortly before midnight, a sailor on lookout spotted something in the darkness. He couldn't really see it. But he knew it could be only one thing—an **iceberg.** An iceberg is a floating mountain of ice that has broken away from a glacier. Hitting an iceberg can damage a ship.

The sailor quickly sounded the alarm: "Iceberg right ahead!" The crew jumped into action. They tried to turn *Titanic* away from the iceberg. But it was too late. The ship scraped along the mountain of ice.

At first, the problem didn't seem too bad. But the iceberg had damaged the ship. Water poured in. Nothing could stop it. Water soon flooded the lowest decks. It kept rising. The crew knew that the unsinkable ship would sink.

The Nightmare Night

Slowly, the wonder ship's nose dipped into the water. Her stern, or back, rose high in the air. In just a few hours, the whole ship would sink. The crew shot off fireworks to tell other ships that *Titanic* needed help.

Sailors on a passing ship spotted the fireworks. They thought the fireworks were part of a celebration, however. So they did not help the sinking ship.

Meanwhile, *Titanic*'s crew began trying to save passengers. Some people quickly ran from their rooms. Many were still in their pajamas. On the main deck, a band played music to calm them. Other people refused to believe there was any real danger.

The ship's crew put people into lifeboats. Women and children mainly went first. But *Titanic* didn't have enough lifeboats for all her passengers. And, in the rush, some lifeboats left with empty seats. After the last boat left, 1,500 people were still aboard the sinking ship.

A little after 2:00 a.m., passengers heard a terrible sound. *Titanic* was ripping apart. People jumped off the doomed ship into the icy water. She vanished into the sea at 2:20 a.m.

Titanic sank more than two miles to the ocean floor. Two-thirds of her 2,200 passengers and crew went down with the ship.

The unsinkable ship that sank lay beneath the Atlantic Ocean for 71 years. Then National Geographic helped an explorer look for her.

Breaking News. *A newsboy sells papers in London. The ship's sinking shocked people around the world.*

Unhappy Ending. *The* Titanic *breaks apart just a few minutes before sinking to the seafloor.*

From the Deep. *Bob Ballard and a crew member sit in their ship's control room. They are watching images of an anchor from* Titanic.

A Boy's Dream

As a kid, scientist Robert Ballard was interested in shipwrecks. He especially loved reading about *Titanic*. "My lifelong dream," he says, "was to find this great ship."

Ballard became an ocean explorer when he grew up. He visited underwater mountains in the middle of the Atlantic. He found giant worms that live in the ocean. And he never forgot his boyhood dream—to find the *Titanic*.

The task seemed impossible. Some people said *Titanic* had been crushed. Others thought she had broken into little pieces. Everyone agreed the ship was far too deep to reach.

But Ballard was determined. In 1985, he and a French scientist took ships to where *Titanic* had sunk. They used high-tech tools to explore the ocean floor. For weeks, they found nothing.

Then they sent down an underwater craft called *Argo*. Its cameras took videos of the ocean floor and sent them up to the ships.

Found It!

Argo searched for several days. Still nothing. Ballard was sure he had failed. Shortly after midnight on September 1, he decided to get some sleep. He really needed it.

Barely an hour later, someone woke him up. Metal objects were showing up on the video screen. These things could only have come from a boat. Soon the team spotted a huge ship engine. They had found the *Titanic*!

Over the next few days, *Argo* circled the wreck. Ballard almost couldn't believe what he saw. *Titanic*'s bow, or front, was stuck in mud. Yet the ship still looked huge.

Ballard also found many sad reminders of *Titanic*'s passengers. He saw beds, suitcases, cups, and countless shoes. It was almost like visiting a sunken museum.

Ballard wanted to see more. But he had run out of time. He had to return home. Before leaving, though, he vowed to come back.

A Closer Look

Ballard kept his promise. In 1986, he rode down to *Titanic* in a tiny **submersible.** And he sent a deep-sea robot, named *J.J.,* into the ship.

As it explored, the robot sent pictures to Ballard. He called *J.J.* a "swimming eyeball."

J.J. glided down *Titanic*'s grand staircase. It peeked into her gym. The robot also gazed at chairs, bowls, and other items on the seafloor.

Before leaving, Ballard wanted to honor the tragic ship. He left a plaque to remember the people who had died. Aside from that, he left everything exactly the way he found it.

Ballard didn't see *Titanic* again for years. He went back in June 2004. He wanted to know how the great ship was doing.

He found that other visitors have really damaged the ship. Submarines have punched holes into *Titanic*'s main deck. And people have taken about 6,000 things from the wreck. These include dishes, lamps, a statue, a safe, and even pieces of the ship herself.

Saving History

Ballard is upset that people have taken things from *Titanic*. He thinks that people should leave the ship alone. He says that taking her things away is like robbing a grave.

But Ballard does want to put cameras around the wreck. That way people can see *Titanic*. And they can remember her short, sad glory.

? *Would you bring objects from* Titanic *to the surface? Why or why not?*

Wordwise

deck: layer of a ship
iceberg: floating mountain of ice
maiden: first
submersible: underwater craft

Titanic Today. *The ship sank 94 years ago. Yet some of her windows are still in one piece.*

Talking With Bob Ba

lard

"I'm more than just the *Titanic* guy," says Bob Ballard. He is right about that. Ballard has explored many parts of the ocean. He has found life in unexpected places. He has studied history by looking at shipwrecks. In this interview, Ballard sheds light on his work.

How did you get interested in ocean exploration?

As a kid, I loved *Twenty Thousand Leagues Under the Sea* by Jules Verne. I wanted to be Captain Nemo and command his submarine. All I could think about was ocean exploration. I wanted to see what was down there!

How did you become an ocean explorer?

I was lucky. I grew up in a smart family. My parents were committed to education. We lived near the Scripps Institution of Oceanography in San Diego, California. I won a scholarship to study there. Later I became a naval officer and an oceanographer, or someone who studies the ocean.

There have been many shipwrecks. What is special about *Titanic*?

Titanic's story fills people with a lot of emotions. At the time, *Titanic* was the largest moving object on Earth. It took two hours to sink. So there was time for drama.

You had a ship full of famous passengers looking for safety. You had the captain telling his officers to "be British." The band played music on the sinking deck. You had people trying to talk or buy their way into lifeboats.

People are fascinated by these stories. They're also curious about how we explored *Titanic*. People like the idea of using robots to learn about the shipwreck.

PRIT VESILIND

Deep Discoveries. ABOVE: *Bob Ballard is an ocean explorer.* LEFT: *Submersibles like ALVIN help Ballard explore the deep ocean.*

Why is it a bad idea to take items from the wreck?

For the same reason you wouldn't take a shovel to Gettysburg [a Civil War battlefield] and start digging for stuff. The place is as powerful as the objects. Seeing the objects in place gives you all sorts of information—about how the ship sank, for example. That information is lost when you haul things up and stick them in glass cases.

What was it like to find *Titanic*? How did you feel?

I had mixed emotions. My mom put it well. When I told her I'd found *Titanic*, she said, "Too bad. You're a great scientist. Now they'll only remember you for finding an old boat." In a way, she was right.

Yet *Titanic* wasn't my most important discovery. Finding life at hydrothermal vents was much bigger. On the other hand, my fame for discovering the ship does give me the opportunity to talk about other things, such as education and exploration.

What are you exploring now?

I'm getting serious about underwater archaeology. I have seven graduate students working with me. We'll basically be camping out in the Black Sea and the Aegean Sea. They're full of ancient shipwrecks to study.

What's the best part of your job?

I've been able to provide for my family and raise my kids. I have fulfilled some of my childhood dreams—and I get to do things others only dream about. I love working with kids, trying to get them interested in science and exploration.

What would you tell kids who want to become ocean explorers?

Get a broad education. Take classes in everything you can. Experiment. Don't fear failure; it can be a great teacher. Fall down, then get back up. Follow your dream!

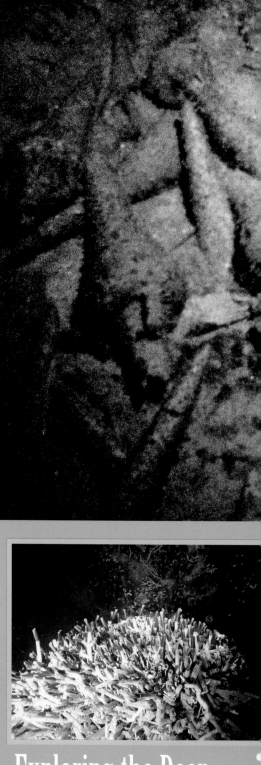

Exploring the Deep

Throughout his career, Ballard has made many important discoveries within the ocean. He found life where no one thought it could exist—around hot cracks on the ocean floor, called hydrothermal vents *(above)*. Today, Ballard explores ancient shipwrecks *(top and right)*. Robot subs help him learn about past cultures.